About This Book

Title: *Gems*

Step: 4

Word Count: 206

Skills in Focus: Soft c and g

Tricky Words: minerals, color, people, jewelry, diamond, opal, emerald, ground, Earth, milky

Ideas For Using This Book

Before Reading:
- **Comprehension:** Look at the title and cover image together. Ask readers what they know about gems. What new things do they think they might learn in the book?
- **Accuracy:** Practice saying the tricky words listed on page 1.
- **Phonemic Awareness:** Tell students they will read words with soft *g* and soft *c* sounds. The letter *g* makes the soft sound /j/ when it is followed by an *e*, *i*, or *y*. The letter *c* makes the soft sound /s/ when it is followed by an *e*, *i*, or *y*. Read the title and remind readers that the *g* in *gems* is soft because it is followed by an *e*. Model how to say each sound in the word *gems* slowly in isolation. Then, blend the sounds together smoothly to say the whole word. Offer additional examples from the book, such as *edges*, *smudges*, and *huge*. Repeat with soft *c* words from the book, such as *face*, *place*, and *nice*.

During Reading:
- Have readers point under each word as they read it.
- **Decoding:** If readers are stuck on a word, help them say each sound and blend the sounds together smoothly. After reading a sentence, point out words with soft *c* and soft *g* as they appear.
- **Comprehension:** Invite readers to talk about new things they are learning about gems while reading. What are they learning that they didn't know before?

After Reading:
Discuss the book. Some ideas for questions:
- What different types of gems have you seen before? What did they look like?
- What do you still wonder about gems?

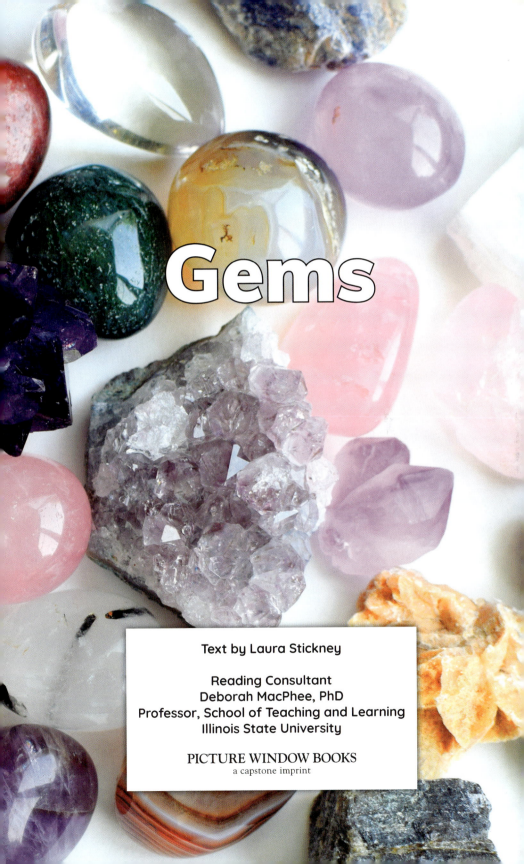

Gems

Text by Laura Stickney

Reading Consultant
Deborah MacPhee, PhD
Professor, School of Teaching and Learning
Illinois State University

PICTURE WINDOW BOOKS
a capstone imprint

What Are Gems?

Gems are a kind of hard, fancy stone. They shine and glint like stars in space.

Gems are minerals.
Minerals make up
Earth's rocks and sand.

They are made deep in the ground in hot places. They take ages to take shape.

People can cut and polish minerals. This makes them into nice gems.

Gems come in a range of colors.

Gems have flat faces and edges called facets.

Gems can be huge or small.

Kinds of Gems

There are many kinds of gems. A ruby is red. Jade and emeralds are nice green gems.

Ruby

Emerald

Opals are milky gems that change color in the sun.

These gems have flecks and smudges of color.

Diamonds can be glassy like ice.

They sell for huge prices at fancy shops.

Pearls are not like other gems.

They are from different places.
These gems form in clam shells.

Rings and Bling

People can make gems into nice jewelry. They cut the gems.

They polish the edges and facets of the gems.

Then they set the gems into necklaces, bracelets, and rings.

They place the gems in metal braces.

You can make nice jewelry with gems.

You can sell diamond wedding rings for a price.

Gems are nice!

More Ideas:

Phonics Activity

Practicing Soft *c* and Soft *g*:
Prepare word cards with story words containing soft and hard *c* and soft and hard *g*. Distribute the cards to the readers. Have students use a marker or highlighter to circle the *c* or *g* in each word. Then have them underline the letter following the *c* or *g* to distinguish whether the *c* or *g* in the word is soft or hard. Have students read the word aloud. They can sort the cards by soft and hard sounds. Words to include:

c words:
- facet
- color
- place
- cut
- fancy
- nice
- clam
- price

g words:
- gem
- glint
- edge
- age
- huge
- smudge
- glossy

Extended Learning Activity

Gem Discovery:
Ask readers to imagine that they have discovered a new kind of gem. Have them draw a picture of the gem on a piece of paper. Then ask readers to write 3–4 sentences about their gem. Challenge students to use soft *c* and soft *g* words in their sentences.

Published by Picture Window Books, an imprint of Capstone
1710 Roe Crest Drive, North Mankato, Minnesota 56003
capstonepub.com

Copyright © 2026 by Capstone.
All rights reserved. No part of this publication may be reproduced in whole or in part, or stored in a retrieval system, or transmitted in any form or by any means, electronic, mechanical, photocopying, recording, or otherwise, without written permission of the publisher.

Library of Congress Cataloging-in-Publication Data is available on the Library of Congress website.

ISBN: 9798875227141 (hardback)
ISBN: 9798875230578 (paperback)
ISBN: 9798875230554 (eBook PDF)

Image Credits: iStock: bonniej, 6, grandriver, 1, 28, Hakase_, 30–31, Liudmila Chernetska, 20–21, magical_light, 8, miljko, 22–23, NickyLloyd, 29, SunChan, 12–13; Shutterstock: Abdul Matloob, 14, Beautyimage, 13, 32, Byjeng, cover, DuxX, 17, EgolenaHK, 4–5, 26–27, IngeBlessas, 15, JGW Images, 18, Kzenon, 24–25, Matteo Gabrieli, 7, MyBestCollection, 10–11, New Africa, 9, 16, Oksana Lyskova, 2–3, Subbotina Anna, 19